BOXER AND BRANDON

بُوكسَر وَ برَانڈون

www.kidkiddos.com

Copyright©2015 by S. A. Publishing ©2017 by KidKiddos Books Ltd.

support@kidkiddos.com

First edition, 2017

Translated from English by Amal Mrissa

قامت بترجمة هذه القصّة من الإنجليزيّة: أمل مريصة

Arabic editing by Fatima Bekkouche

Library and Archives Canada Cataloguing in Publication Data

Boxer and Brandon (Arabic Bilingual Edition)

ISBN: 978-1-5259-0631-2 paperback

ISBN: 978-1-5259-0632-9 hardcover

ISBN: 978-1-5259-0630-5 eBook

Please note that the Arabic and English versions of the story have been written to be as close as possible. However, in some cases they differ in order to accommodate nuances and fluidity of each language.

KidKiddos Books

Inna Nusinsky

للكَاتِبَةِ إيــنّا نُونْسِينْسْكِي

Illustrations by Gillian Tolentino

الرّسوم: جيليان تولنتينو

Hello, my name is Boxer. I'm a boxer. I'm a type of dog called a boxer. Nice to meet you! This is the story of how I got my new family.

مَرْحَبًا، اِسْمِي بُوكْسَرْ. أَنَا أَنْتَمِي إِلَى نَوْعٍ مِنَ الْكِلَابِ يُدْعَى بُوكْسَرْ، سَعِدْتُ بِمَعْرِفَتِكُمْ كَثِيرًا. هَذِهِ قِصَّتِي، إِقْرَؤُوهَا حَتَّى تَكْتَشِفُوا كَيْفَ تَعَرَّفْتُ عَلَى أُسْرَتِي الْجَدِيدَةِ.

It all started when I was two years old. I was homeless. I lived on the street and ate out of garbage cans.

بدَأَ كُلُّ شَيْءٍ عِنْدَمَا كَانَ عُمْرِي عَامَيْنِ. كُنْتُ مُشَرَّدًا أَعِيشُ فِي الشَّوَارِعِ وَ أَقْتَاتُ مِنَ صَنَادِيقِ القُمَامَةِ.

People got pretty mad at me when I knocked over their trash cans. "Get out of here!" they would shout.

كَانَ النَّاسُ يَغْضَبُونَ مِنِّي كَثِيرا عِنْدَمَا كُنْتُ أَرْتَمِي عَلَى صَنَادِيقِ القُمَامَةِ الخَاصَّةِ بِهِمْ فَأُسْقِطُهَا، وكَانُوا يَصْرُخُونَ قَائِلِينَ:" اُغْرُبْ عَن وَجْهِي!"

Sometimes I had to run away really fast!

وَ فِي بَعْضِ الأَحْيَانِ، كَانَ عَلَيَّ أَنْ أَهْرُبَ بِسُرْعَةٍ كَبِيرَةٍ خَوْفًا مِنْهُمْ.

Living in the city can be hard.

الحَيَاةُ فِي المَدِينَةِ صَعْبَةٌ أَحْيَانًا.

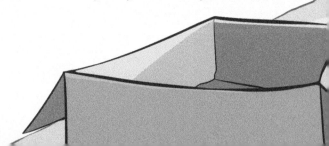

When I wasn't looking for food, I liked to sit and watch people walk by on the sidewalk.

عِنْدَمَا لَمْ أَكُنْ أَبْحَثُ عَنِ الطَّعَامِ، كُنْتُ أُحِبُّ الْجُلُوسَ عَلَى قَارِعَةِ الطَّرِيقِ و مُشَاهَدَةَ النَّاسِ يَسِيرُونَ عَلَى الرَّصِيفِ.

Sometimes, I would look at people with my sad eyes and they would give me food.

وكُنْتُ فِي بَعْضِ الْأَحْيَانِ أَنْظُرُ إِلَيْهِمْ بِعَيْنَيْنِ حَزِينَتَيْنِ فَيَحِنُّ قَلْبُهُمْ و يُطْعِمُونَنِي.

"Oh, what a cute doggy! Here, have a snack," they would say.

وكَانُوا يَقُولُونَ لِي مَثَلاً: " آه، يَالَكَ مِنْ كَلْب لَطِيف إِلَيْكَ بَعْضَ الطَّعَامِ."

One day, a little boy and his dad were walking toward me. "How's that sandwich, Brandon?" asked the boy's dad.

و فِي يَوْمٍ مِنَ الْأَيَّامِ، كَانَ طِفْلٌ صَغِيرٌ و وَالِدُهُ يَسِيرَانِ فِي اتِّجَاهِي، فَسَأَلَ الْأَبُ الطِّفْلَ: " هَلْ أَعْجَبَتْكَ الشَّطِيرَةُ يَا بْرَانْدُونْ؟"

The sandwich looked really good!

و بَدَتِ الشَّطِيرَةُ شَهِيَّةً جِدّاً!

I put on my sad eyes. The boy stopped and held out his sandwich. I was just about to take a bite, when...

نَظَرْتُ إِلَيْهِمَا بِعَيْنَيْنِ بَائِسَتَيْنِ، فَتوقَّفَ الوَلَدُ وَ مَدَّ إِلَيَّ شَطِيرَتَهُ. كِدْتُ أَنْ آخُذَ قَضْمَةً لَوْلَا...

"Brandon, don't feed that dog! He'll just come looking for more," exclaimed his dad. Brandon pulled the sandwich back.

قَالَ الأَبُ نَاهِرًا:" لَا تُطْعِمْ ذَلِكَ الكَلْبَ يَا بْرَانْدُونْ! سَيُلَاحِقُنَا طَلَبًا لِلْمَزِيدِ." فَسَحَبَ بْرَانْدُونْ الشَّطِيرَةَ مِنِّي.

So close—I could smell the butter! Parents never want to share with me!

عِنْدَمَا كُنْتُ قَرِيبًا مِنَ الشَّطِيرَةِ، اسْتَطَعْتُ أَنْ أَشُمَّ الزُّبْدَ. مِنَ المُحْزِنِ حَقًّا أَنَّ الآبَاءَ يَرْفُضُونَ أَنْ يَقْتَسِمُوا طَعَامَهُمْ مَعِي!

I whined as pitifully as I could as they walked away.

وَ مِنْ شِدَّةِ حُزْنِي، أَنَّيْتُ بِصَوْتٍ عَالٍ بَيْنَمَا سَارَ الاثْنَانِ بَعِيدًا.

After that, I decided to take a nap. I was having a wonderful dream. I was in a park and everything was made from meat! The trees were steaks! It was the best dream ever.

و بَعْدَ ذَلِكَ ، قَرَّرْتُ أَنْ آخَذَ قَيْلُولَةً ، و كَانَتْ قَيْلُولَتِي تِلْكَ مَلِيئَةً بِحُلْمٍ رَائِعٍ ، فَقَدْ كُنْتُ في مُنْتَزَهٍ كُلُّ شَيْءٍ فيهِ مَصْنُوعٌ مِنَ اللَّحْمِ فَكَانَتِ الْأَشْجَارُ مِثْلَ شَرَائِحِ لَحْمٍ شَهِيَّةٍ لَقَدْ كَانَ ذَلِكَ أَفْضَلَ حُلْمٍ عَلَى الْإِطْلَاقِ.

Something woke me up, though. Right in front of me was a piece of a sandwich! I jumped to my feet and gobbled it down.

وَلَكِنَّ شَيْئًا مَا أيْقَظَني مِنَ النَّوْمِ ، فَقَدْ وَجَدْتُ أمَامِي قِطْعَةً مِنْ شَطِيرَةٍ فَقَفَزْتُ مِنْ مَكَانِي و الْتَهَمْتُهَا .

Mmmmm! It was so good! Just like my dream.

مممم! لَقَدْ كَانَتْ لَذِيذَةً جِدًّا مِثْلَ حُلْمِي.

"Shhh," said Brandon. "Don't tell Dad." *What a nice little boy*, I thought to myself.

قَالَ برَانْدُونْ " هُسْ ، لَا تُخْبِرْ أبِي ." فَقُلْتُ فِي نَفْسِي :" يَالَهُ مِنْ وَلَدٍ طَيِّبٍ."

Day after day, Brandon would come visit me and give me a snack. Then, one day...

و يَوْمًا بَعْدَ يَوْمٍ، كَانَ بْرَانْدُونْ يَزُورُنِي لِيُطْعِمَنِي ، و لَكِنْ ، فِي يَوْمٍ مِنَ الْأيَّامِ....

"Hurry up, Brandon. You'll be late for school," said Brandon's dad.

قَالَ وَالِدُ بْرَانْدُونْ :" أَسْرِعْ يَا بْرَانْدُونْ ، فَسَتَتَأَخَّرُ عَنِ الْمَدْرَسَةِ ."

"I'm coming!" shouted Brandon as he ran past, dropping a brown bag on the sidewalk.

فَصَاحَ بْرَانْدُونْ: " أَنَا آتٍ! " و رَكَضَ مُسْرِعًا، فَأَسْقَطَ كِيسًا بُنِّيًّا عَلَى الرَّصِيفِ.

Sniffing around, I walked up to it and looked inside. It was full of food!

فَتَوَجَّهْتُ نَحْوَ الْكِيسِ و شَمَمْتُهُ ، ثُمَّ نَظَرْتُ إِلَى مَا بِدَاخِلِهِ ، فَكَانَ مَلِيئًا بِالطَّعَامِ.

I was just about to eat it all when I thought of something. *Brandon always brings me food when I'm hungry. If I eat his food, then he'll be hungry.*

كِدْتُ أَنْ أَلْتَهِمَهُ كُلَّهُ لَوْلَا أَنْ قُلْتُ فِي نَفْسِي :" إنَّ برانْدُونْ دَائِمًا مَا يَجِيءُ لِي بِالطَّعَامِ عِنْدَمَا أَكُونُ جَائِعًا . فَإِذَا أَكَلْتُ طَعَامَهُ ، سَيَشْعُرُ هُوَ بِالْجُوعِ."

"I'm coming, Brandon!"
I howled. He and his dad were
way down the street. I ran after
them with the brown bag in my
mouth.

فَعَوَيْتُ: " أَنَا آتٍ يا بْرَانْدُونْ" و كَانَ بْرَانْدُونْ و
وَالِدُهُ بَعِيدَيْنِ عَنِّي، فَرَكَضْتُ خَلْفَهُمَا و الْكِيسُ
الْبُنِّيُّ فِي فَمِي.

As I was passing an alleyway, I saw a cat. I hate cats! I forgot about my mission and dropped the bag.

وَبَيْنَما كُنْتُ أَجْتازُ مَمَرًّا ، لَمَحْتُ قِطًّا . كَمْ أَكْرَهُ الْقِطَطَا! فَنَسِيتُ مُهِمَّتِي وَ أَسْقَطْتُ الْكِيسَ مِنْ فَمِي.

"Bark, get out of here, cat!" I barked.

وَ نَبَحْتُ :" اِرْحَلْ مِنْ هُنَا أَيُّهَا الْقِطُّ! "

Then I remembered Brandon's lunch. He was going to be hungry if I didn't bring him his lunch!

ثُمَّ تَذَكَّرْتُ فَطُورَ بَرَانْدُونْ وَكَيْفَ أَنَّهُ سَيَجُوعُ إِذَا لَمْ أُحْضِرْ لَهُ طَعَامَهُ!

It was hard, but I forgot about the cat. I picked up the brown bag again and started running.

لَقَدْ كَانَ ذَلِكَ صَعْبًا ، وَلَكِنَّنِي نَسِيتُ أَمْرَ الْقِطِّ ، فَالْتَقَطْتُ الْكِيسَ مُجَدَّدًا وَ بَدَأْتُ بِالرَّكْضِ.

Further down the street, I stopped again. A butcher shop!

وَ فِي طَرِيقِي تَوَقَّفْتُ مُجَدَّدًا عِنْدَمَا رَأَيْتُ مَتْجَرَ جَزَّارٍ.

There were pieces of meat and sausages hanging everywhere. Mmmmm...

لَقَدْ كَانَتْ هُنَالِكَ قِطَعٌ مِنَ اللَّحْمِ وَ النَّقَانِقِ مُعَلَّقَةً فِي كُلِّ مَكَانٍ، يَمممم...

Wait! I had to bring Brandon his lunch or he was going to be hungry!

وَ لَكِنْ مَهْلاً! عَلَيَّ أَنْ أُحْضِرَ لِبْرَانْدُونْ غَذَاءَهُ وَ إِلَّا سَيَشْعُرُ بِالجُوعِ!

It was hard, but I forgot about the meat. I grabbed the lunch and started running again.

كَانَ ذَلِكَ صَعْبًا، وَلَكِنَّنِي نَسِيتُ أَمْرَ اللَّحْمِ وَ الْتَقَطْتُ كِيسَ الغَذَاءِ قَبْلَ أَنْ أَبْدَأَ بِالرَّكْضِ مُجَدَّدًا.

I turned a corner and stopped. There was another dog wagging his tail.

انْعَطَفْتُ رَاكِضًا ثُمَّ تَوَقَّفْتُ، فَقَدْ وَجَدْتُ كَلْبًا آخَرَ يَهُزُّ ذَيْلَهُ.

"Hi, want to play?" he woofed.

قَالَ الكَلْبُ:" أَهْلاً، أَتُرِيدُ أَنْ تَلْعَبَ مَعِي؟"

"I sure do!" I answered. "Oh, wait, I can't right now. I have to bring Brandon his lunch."

فَأَجَبْتُهُ بِحَمَاسٍ:" طَبْعًا أُرِيدُ!" ثُمَّ تَرَدَّدْتُ قَائِلًا:"مَهْلًا، لَا أَسْتَطِيعُ أَنْ أَلْعَبَ مَعَكَ الآنَ، عَلَيَّ أَنْ أُوصِلَ لِبْرَانْدُونْ غَذَاءَهُ."

It was hard, but I forgot about playing. I grabbed the lunch and started running again.

وَكَانَ ذَلِكَ صَعْبًا، وَ لَكِنَّني نَسِيتُ أَمْرَ اللَّعِبِ وَ الْتَقَطْتُ كِيسَ الغَذَاءِ وَ بَدَأْتُ بِالرَّكْضِ مُجَدَّدًا.

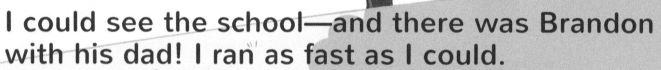

I could see the school—and there was Brandon with his dad! I ran as fast as I could.

أَصْبَحْتُ قَرِيبًا مِنَ الْمَدْرَسَةِ – وَ اسْتَطَعْتُ أَيْضًا أَنْ أَلْمَحَ بْرَانْدُونْ مَعَ وَالِدِهِ، فَوَاصَلْتُ الرَّكْضَ بِأَقْصَى سُرْعَتِي.

Stopping in front of Brandon, I dropped his lunch bag on the sidewalk. Just in time!

تَوَقَّفْتُ أَمَامَ بْرَانْدُونْ؛ ثُمَّ وَضَعْتُ كِيسَ غَذَائِهِ عَلَى الرَّصِيفِ. مِنْ حُسْنِ الْحَظِّ أَنَّني وَصَلْتُ فِي الْوَقْتِ تَمَامًا!

"Look, Dad, he brought my lunch!" exclaimed Brandon.

قَالَ بْرَنْدُونْ مُتَعَجِّبًا:" انْظُرْ يَا أَبِي، لَقَدْ أَحْضَرَ لِي غَذَائِي!"

"Wow, he sure did. That's amazing!" said his dad. They both patted me on the head.

فَقَالَ الْأَبُ:" وَاوْ، لَقَدْ فَعَلَ ذَلِكَ حَقًا. هَذَا رَائِعٌ!" ثُمَّ رَبَّتَ الْاِثْنَانِ عَلَى رَأْسِي.

Brandon was happy and so was his dad.

شَعَرَ بْرَانْدُونْ وَ وَالِدُهُ بِالفَرْحَةِ.

In fact, his dad was so happy that he brought me home. He gave me a bath. He gave me food!

وَ فِي الوَاقِعِ، كَانَ وَالِدُهُ فَرِحًا جِدًّا إِلَى دَرَجَةِ أَنَّهُ أَخَذَنِي إِلَى بَيْتِهِ وَ حَمَّمَنِي وَ أَطْعَمَنِي.

Now when Brandon and his dad go walking, I get to walk with them. And when they go home, I get to go home with them!

وَ الآنَ، كُلَّمَا خَرَجَ بْرَانْدُونْ وَ وَالِدُهُ لِلمَشْيِ، أُرَافِقُهُمَا. وَ عِنْدَمَا يَعُودَانِ إِلَى الْبَيْتِ، أَعُودُ مَعَهُمَا.

I love my new home and my new family!

أَنَا أُحِبُّ مَنْزِلِي الْجَدِيدَ وَ عَائِلَتِي الْجَدِيدَةَ!